WITHDRAWN
VMI LIBRARY

About the Author

Ray Bethers is first of all a painter, although his several books on art reveal an unusual talent for clarifying a subject which is very often confusing to layman and student. Born in Oregon, Ray Bethers attended the University of Oregon, the California School of Fine Arts, the Art Students League of New York, and has studied in Paris. He has served on the Board of Directors of the California School of Fine Arts and has been an art instructor. He is the winner of the Pennell Purchase Prize in wood engraving and has painted in Europe, South and Central America, Mexico, and in the South Seas. As this book goes to press he is painting in Paris.

HOW PAINTINGS HAPPEN

By RAY BETHERS

with Diagrams by the Author

W · W · NORTON & COMPANY · INC · New York

COPYRIGHT 1951 BY RAY BETHERS

FIRST EDITION

PRINTED IN THE UNITED STATES OF AMERICA
FOR THE PUBLISHERS BY THE VAIL-BALLOU PRESS

CONTENTS

Acknowledgment	9
How Paintings Happen	13
What Can Be Expected from a Work of Art	14
The Relative Importance of Subject Matter	15
Art as Communication	15
Imagination in Painting	15
What Is Abstraction?	17
Art Is Not a Copy of Nature	17
The Necessity for Pictorial Space	18
The Arts and Time	19
The Effect of Shape on Pictures	20
Line Directions as Emotional Symbols	20
Pictures Are Painted on the Picture Plane	22
The Spatial Effect of the Picture Plane	22
Pictorial Space versus Mechanical Perspective	23
Movement on and behind the Picture Plane	23
Arrangement or Pictorial Composition	24
Pattern Is Flat and Lies on the Surface	24
The Combination of Pattern with Pictorial Space	25
Line Directions in Pattern and Space	26
The Importance of Color Values	28
Functional Color in Painting	28
The Effect of Textures	28
Thought and Feeling	28
How to Look at the Pictures that Follow	29
The Comparison of Paintings with Their Motif Photographs	31
Israel Litwak: TIMES SQUARE	33
Frederick Franck: TIMES SQUARE	35

Frederick Franck: CANNES	37
Stow Wengenroth: BROOKLYN BRIDGE	39
Louis Guglielmi: MENTAL GEOGRAPHY	40
Joseph Stella: BROOKLYN BRIDGE	41
Hazard Durfee: SALT WATER FARM	43
Armin Landeck: SKETCH FOR "14TH STREET ROOFTOP"	45
Armin Landeck: 14TH STREET ROOFTOP (DRY POINT)	46
Armin Landeck: 14TH STREET ROOFTOP (OIL)	47
David Fredenthal: ROOFTOPS NO. 1	49
David Fredenthal: FLIGHT OVER ROOFTOPS	50
David Fredenthal: SUMMER RAIN	51
David Fredenthal: WIND AND SUN	52
David Fredenthal: STRIVING CITY	53
Dorothy Andrews: GREENWICH VILLAGE PASSAGEWAY	55
Victor Arnautoff: CALIFORNIA LANDSCAPE	57
Revington Arthur: FARM NEAR CHAUTAUQUA	59
Morris Blackburn: RED SUMMER SUN	61
Aaron Bohrod: LANDSCAPE, SOUTHERN ILLINOIS	63
Jean de Botton: STILL LIFE WITH THE SPINET	64
Jean de Botton: LES COURSES À LONGCHAMPS—PARIS	65
Louis Bouché: PONY RIDE	67
Alexander Brook: HICK'S ISLAND	69
Nicolai Cikovsky: SHINNECOCK HILLS	71
Howard Cook: RIO GRANDE	73
Russell Cowles: THE DICTATOR	75
Lamar Dodd: FACTOR'S WALK	77
Stephen Etnier: LATE AFTERNOON	79
Dean Fausett: AUTUMN IN NEW ENGLAND	81
Ruth Gikow: LOW TIDE	83
Louis Guglielmi: OBSOLETE STRUCTURE	85
John Haley: PENITENTE COUNTRY	87
Eric Isenburger: ROMAN WALLS	89
Bernard Karfiol: THE COVE	91
Karl Kasten: THE EMBARCADERO	93

Dong Kingman: CITY HALL IN WHITE 95
Georgina Klitgaard: ARBOR DAY AT THE SCHOOL 97
Karl Knaths: TIDE WASH 99
Yasuo Kuniyoshi: HEADLESS HORSE WHO WANTS TO JUMP 101
Irving Lehman: FOG—BOWLING GREEN 103
John Chapman Lewis: THE BRIDGE 105
Ward Lockwood: THE VALLEY BELOW 107
Erle Loran: ROCK EQUILIBRIUM 109
Luigi Lucioni: THE THREE GRACES 111
Nan Lurie: LIGHT AND SHADE UNDER THE EL 113
John Marin: WOOLWORTH BUILDING, NEW YORK, NO. 3 115
Jose Moya del Pino: TREES, SEA AND ROCKS 117
Georgia O'Keeffe: RANCHOS CHURCH 119
Arthur Osver: NOCTURNE 121
Robert Philipp: GLOUCESTER HARBOR 123
Waldo Peirce: BACK YARD 125
Steve Raffo: CITY SUNSET 127
Zoltan Sepeshy: MORNING 129
Benton Spruance: WINTER MOONLIGHT 131
Reuben Tam: NORTHERN TERRAIN 133
John Taylor: THE TOWER 135
Glenn Wessels: OREGON COAST 137
Sol Wilson: CHURCH ACROSS THE BAY 139
Karl Zerbe: BRIDGE 141
Jean Xceron: LINE VARIATIONS NO. 1 143

All Pictures Are Not for All People 145
Index 147

ACKNOWLEDGMENT

This book has been made possible through the co-operation of many painters. Not only did these artists send photographs of their paintings, they also sent photographs of the *place where they painted their pictures*. In almost every instance these motif photographs were taken later, for few painters ever *photograph* the subjects they paint. Many of these motifs were difficult to photograph. With Karl Knaths, for instance, "three things had to happen at the same time. A photographer who works at something else having a free moment, the sun to shine, the tide to be out. It finally happened."

Each painter has also written on his attitude toward nature Most painters will tell you that words are not their medium of expression, but I think you'll find their words expressive, clear, and illuminating. The originals of these letters are now in the Collection of American Literature at Yale University.

I hope my sincere feeling of gratitude toward these painters will be seconded by everyone who reads this book.

My own point of view as expressed on the following pages parallels that of my three former books, *Pictures, Painters, and You, Composition in Pictures,* and *From Eye to Camera.* All were published by the Pitman Publishing Corporation, New York.

Ray Bethers
New York

HOW
PAINTINGS
HAPPEN

A work of art must be born in obscurity, must vacillate and search in feeling out its direction.

—ANDRÉ LHOTE

ART IS NOT A COPY OF NATURE

How Paintings Happen

This book is dedicated to the proposition (as far as art is concerned) that all men are *not* created equal. Democracy in art is not the necessity for artists to please large numbers of people, but the right of each painter to paint as *he* chooses, with a corresponding freedom of choice by all who look at pictures. In other words, all pictures can never be for all people. In addition, here are four other basic premises inherent in this book:

1. Art is *not* a copy of nature.
2. Art conveys emotion rather than information.
3. Painting is a medium of expression in its own right and cannot be translated into words.
4. Painting as a fine art is made possible partly through its inherent limitations of actual space and time.

This book is in reality four books in one, all parts related and yet all parts different.

First are the author's words and diagrams to help explain the structure of pictures. These you will find in the first section, as well as continued beneath each painting. The brief comments on the paintings attempt to explain certain elements that help to organize and unify the particular pictures. They are *not* intended in any way to point out the painting's best features, for sometimes only minor aspects are discussed, related more to the plan of the book than to their relative importance in the specific painting.

Second are the motif photographs which match each painting, to show *what* it was in "nature" that prompted each painter to *begin* his picture.

Third are the paintings, which are complete in themselves, and fourth, the painters' attitudes toward nature, expressed in the painters' own words.

Most of the paintings shown are landscapes, but the principles involved will apply equally well to paintings of all kinds.

The total meaning in this book is directed not only to students and painters, but also to anyone who wishes to understand and appreciate painting as a fine art. You will find no painting "rules" in this book, for the only rules in art are that *art cannot be defined* and that *all rules can be broken*. And since it is possible that some of the paintings shown are not great works of art, you will have the opportunity to decide which ones you feel are.

What Can Be Expected from a Work of Art

A painting as a work of art does not *provide* an emotional experience, it only offers an opportunity for this experience if we are able and willing to accept it.

In looking at pictures, there are many things to *know* as well as to feel, for although art will always be mysterious, there are many qualities which have been repeated in pictures since painting began.

Order and variety, for instance, are fundamental to creative pictures but have little meaning in themselves without the addition of an artist's personal feeling. Pictures are also complete within themselves—they need no explanatory titles of any kind—and have a unique quality for renewing themselves, which gives them a life of their own. They also offer an opportunity for creative participation, for the observer is also part of the picture. In addition, there is no particular subject matter that is aesthetically better than another; otherwise, artists could be judged on their merit as "subject choosers." This does not mean, of course, that *you* might not prefer one subject to another.

What you can expect from a painting as a work of art is actually intangible. It is emotional, personal, and *impossible* to describe in words. And yet when an aesthetic experience happens, it *is* tangible—but only to *you*.

The Relative Importance of Subject Matter

The relationship of subject matter to a work of art is generally misunderstood, for the subject of a picture (if it has one) is usually more important to the painter than to the picture he paints.

As an example of this fact, let us suppose that a painter feels deeply about certain political conditions which he would like to change. This he sets out to do by painting a satirical picture, but in the meantime this political situation clears up of its own accord. Now, with no longer any *political* justification for his work, should the picture be destroyed?

There is no definite answer to this question. If the picture *depends* entirely on its subject matter, it may still have historic interest. But should the painting turn out to be a work of art, it cannot help but live in *spite* of the outdated cause which inspired it.

Subject matter is primarily important in that it may be the incentive for *beginning* a picture, but from then on it moves into the realm of art and can no longer be considered from its former actual world relationships.

Art as Communication

Art has often been described as a form of communication, but the question is—what kind of communication?

Many pictures communicate information. The *events* shown in news photographs can interest a great many people. This interest, however, is seldom in the photograph *as a picture,* but only in the *events* taking place in the picture.

Paintings as works of art also communicate but in a far different way. In painting, the *entire picture* is the event, for an intangible emotional communication can be derived from the picture as a whole.

Imagination in Painting

Painters do not actually *see* any differently from anyone else. Someone once asked Matisse how he *saw* an orange. His answer was, "That depends on whether I am buying it, eating it, or painting it."

Imagination is not the creation of something entirely new, but is only the combination of the known in new relationships. So far, it seems to have been impossible for man to imagine anything outside his own visual experience. Legendary animals such as unicorns, for instance, are nothing more than horses with an added horn, while dragons are a combination of claws, legs, teeth, and so on, taken from other known animals, birds, and reptiles.

DEGREES OF ABSTRACTION

What Is Abstraction?

This word "abstraction" has many meanings, even when applied to painting.

As used here and throughout this book, abstraction means the departure *away* from nature—the farther away from nature, the greater the *degree* of abstraction.

Progressive degrees of abstraction (away from nature) are shown from left to right in the first three diagrams. Since the fourth diagram has departed *completely* from nature, we can call it a pure abstraction. "Non-objective" is only another name for pure abstraction.

Degree of abstraction has little to do with relative excellence in pictures, however, for works of art can be found in any degree.

Art Is Not a Copy of Nature

For the purposes of this book, nature is the three-dimensional world about us, extending through space in all directions. There is little about this three-dimensional world that is absolute, however, for nature, like painting, is always perceived through personal feeling, knowledge, and past experience. Even so, the one fact that art is always made *by* man *for* man should tell us that art *isn't* nature and that nature *isn't* art.

Artists have always gone to nature for source material, and the reasons for this are obvious. It is primarily because the endless *variety* of nature (aside from its inspirational effect) helps to prevent an artist from repeating himself. For as soon as a painter repeats what he has already done, he is a copyist and no longer an artist.

The words *emotion* and *feeling* will occur often in this book but will seldom be found on the next few pages, which are meant to be as unemotional as possible. These unemotional words and diagrams are intended to provide a kind of visual alphabet of the basic structure of pictures, for pictures, like musical compositions, poetry, and all other art forms, must have some kind of formal organization which clarifies apprehension and makes emotional expression possible. This "visual alphabet" may be difficult to understand at first, but you have probably forgotten the amount of time you once spent in learning the *letters of the alphabet* which are now lost in the *ideas* contained in words.

So, with emotion temporarily left behind, let us begin our "alphabet" with the fact that nature has *three* dimensions—while painting has but *two*.

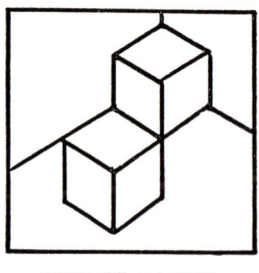 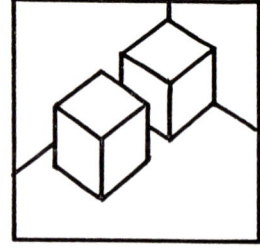

COPY OF NATURE   PICTORIAL SPACE

The Necessity for *Pictorial* Space

The cubes in the diagram on the left have been "copied from nature" just as they appear to the human eye. In other words, they have been accurately transferred from the *three* dimensions of the actual world to the *two* dimensions of the world of pictures.

In the actual space of the actual world, the changing focus of your *two* eyes as "seen" through your mind tells you the truth about spatial relationships. But everything in this diagram is on only *one* plane (which the unchanging focus of your eyes will confirm) while the two cubes are placed in such a way that your mind cannot establish their spatial relationships. Since their positions appear to fluctuate in space, what can be done to make these relative positions clearly understood? This is shown in the second diagram, where it has been necessary to tell a lie in order to approximate the truth (the position of one cube has been changed). This diagram shows how the *overlapping* of objects drawn on a flat plane will convey the *feeling* of space to the eyes and mind. This *feeling* of space in painting can also be achieved in many other ways. But in all painting some method must be found to give the feeling of space where there is no space.

This necessity for *pictorial* space is not actually a limitation, for it offers one of the many opportunities for creative expression in painting.

STATIC

PICTORIAL MOVEMENT

The Arts and Time

Time is also a dimension of the actual world, for it requires actual time for trees to *sway*, birds to *fly*, and cloud shadows to move over the landscape.

It also takes actual time to read these words, for words, like notes in music, must always follow one another in sequence over a period of actual time.

The inherent sequential order and movement through actual time make compositions possible in both literature and music. But in pictures there is *no movement* nor any inherent order for seeing the parts in sequence. Pictures are always seen as a whole, with all parts seen simultaneously.

This limitation of the time element in pictures is only an apparent limitation for it is one of the qualities which makes painting different from other art forms. Lack of movement must be approximated by composing pictures so that attention is directed throughout in an orderly and interesting manner. In this way confusion can be eliminated, pictures will appear complete rather than fragmentary, and the feeling of movement in the actual world can be implied.

These two diagrams show how lack of movement and the feeling of movement can be suggested within a picture's frame.

This static quality of painting is also one of the reasons why storytelling pictures sometimes appear trite, for stories are best told through literature, in plays, or in *moving* pictures, where suspense can be sustained until the unforeseen climax at the very end.

Stopped action in painting may also fail to be convincing if not integrated into the movement of the picture as a whole. Otherwise action will appear to be "frozen," like the fragmentary effect of an isolated motion-picture frame.

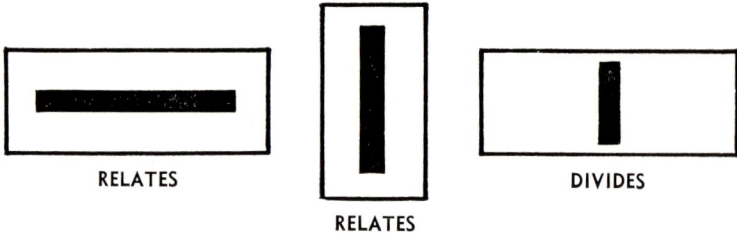

The Effect of Shape on Pictures

Think of the *format* of a picture as its *frame*, for the format is a picture's shape.

Most painters begin their compositions on an already established format, for each line, form, and direction cannot help but be affected by the particular format's size and proportions as well as by its vertical and horizontal boundary lines. This does not mean that a predetermined format may not change as a picture develops, however, as an artist must always feel free to change his picture in any way at any time.

The shapes in the first and second diagrams are in relation to their particular formats where each shape accents and repeats its format's dominant direction.

The shape in the third diagram is *not* in relation, however, for it does not unify but *divides* its format into two parts.

Line Directions as Emotional Symbols

Line directions, although not descriptive of tangible objects in the actual world, can nevertheless produce an emotional effect from their dominant directions alone. The reactions to these emotional effects is deep-rooted in the human race, for they all originate in human experience.

Vertical directions. These have an inherent feeling of dignity such as we feel on seeing tall buildings, tall trees, or even tall people.

Horizontal directions. The emotional effect of the actual horizon and of horizontal lines is very similar, for horizontal directions are usually quiet and restful. However, horizontal lines can also be used to suggest speed.

Diagonal directions. A diagonal (when parallel to the picture plane) is a falling line midway between the static dignity of the vertical and the horizontal which has already come to rest.

Opposed diagonals. These lines are stable, for they brace one another in pictures just as they do in actual life. However, they are sometimes used to express conflict.

The triangle. The feeling of strength in a triangle (on a horizontal base) is similar in both pictures and architecture. But turn a triangle upside down and it will immediately become unstable.

The circle. A circle is complete in itself, without accent, beginning, or end. This completeness tends to isolate circles in pictures, making them difficult to integrate with other forms.

Curving directions. Curves can be opulent, rhythmic, or even suggest sadness, as in the drooping effect of weeping willow trees.

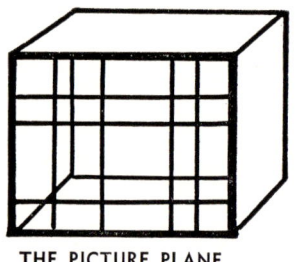 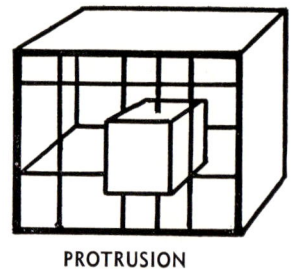

THE PICTURE PLANE   PROTRUSION

Pictures Are Painted <u>on</u> the Picture Plane

The *picture plane* is the flat surface on which pictures are painted. Do not confuse the picture plane with the format, which is *only* a picture's shape.

Paintings are seen *through* the picture plane, the *flatness* of which is the key to all directions and spatial positions *behind* the picture plane. The picture plane can also be compared with a theater proscenium where everything behind it is no longer in the world of actuality but is now in the realm of art.

The first diagram shows a line pattern *on* the picture plane with a purposely *limited* amount of pictorial space shown in the picture box behind.

The second diagram demonstrates the unpleasant illusion of a *broken* picture plane, where a cube is apparently protruding into the actual space of the room.

You will seldom find protrusion in a work of art, nor will you often find the opposite effect of *unlimited* space *behind* the picture plane.

The Spatial Effect of the Picture Plane

The horizontal and vertical boundaries of the picture plane will affect all spatial positions in pictures. This can easily be seen by comparing these two diagrams where both cubes are essentially the same. To do this, twist the book page until the second diagram is horizontal, which will automatically change the position of the cube in space.

Most painters have the ability to see the actual world through an imaginary picture plane, which becomes an exploratory method for selecting subject matter for pictures.

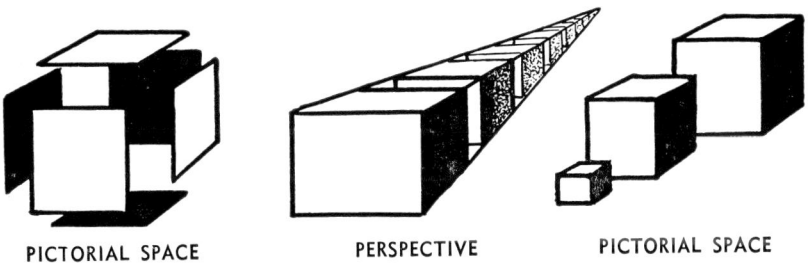

PICTORIAL SPACE   PERSPECTIVE   PICTORIAL SPACE

Pictorial Space versus Mechanical Perspective

Pictorial space gives the *feeling* of space rather than the illusion of it. This is suggested by the "exploded" cube at the left.

The central diagram shows the converging lines and diminishing sizes of mechanical perspective. This produces a visually untrue illusion, aside from the fact that perspective is an inflexible system which most painters find difficult to control.

The third diagram demonstrates how the *overlapping* of forms (in pictorial space) will indicate recession, even though sizes *increase* as they recede.

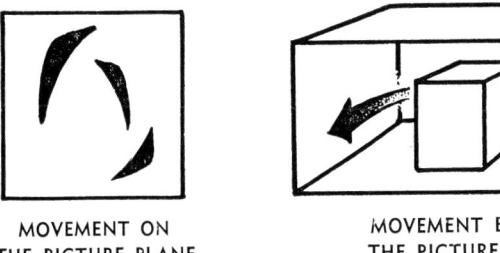

MOVEMENT ON   MOVEMENT BEHIND
THE PICTURE PLANE   THE PICTURE PLANE

Movement on and behind the Picture Plane

Movement can be suggested *on* the picture plane, as shown in the first diagram, or can be directed into and out of space, as indicated in the second diagram. Movement can also be combined in both pattern and space.

In spatial movement the solid forms and empty spaces are equally important, for movement can be directed *through* solid masses as well as through empty space.

[23]

Arrangement or Pictorial Composition

Arrangement in pictures is the direct translation to a flat plane of objects in their actual world relationships. This approach is sometimes useful and necessary in painting informational or factual pictures.

Pictorial composition is quite different, for it is the *unification* (through personal feeling) of an entire picture. In pictorial composition, objects or forms are related to the format, to each other, and to pattern and space on and behind the picture plane.

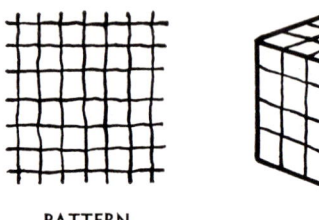
PATTERN

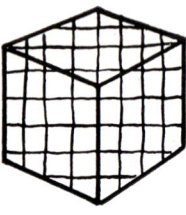

Pattern Is Flat and Lies <u>on</u> the Surface

Pattern is flat and lies on the surface of an object. As used on furniture, for instance, pattern decorates the surface without destroying the form. In this use, pattern is intended to be decorative and pleasing, but with little emotional effect.

The use of pattern in painting is quite different, for although it can also be decorative, its primary function is to preserve the flatness of the picture plane.

The first diagram shows a *flat* pattern of horizontal and vertical lines.

The second diagram illustrates how pattern lies flat as it preserves the surface of an object.

The third diagram, however, explains how pattern can be used creatively in painting where its two-dimensional quality is used to flatten the effect of three dimensions in pictorial space.

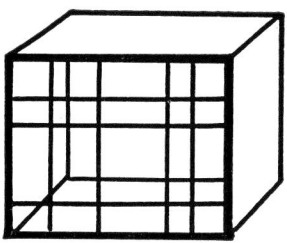

1. PATTERN

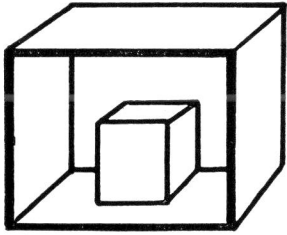

2. PICTORIAL SPACE

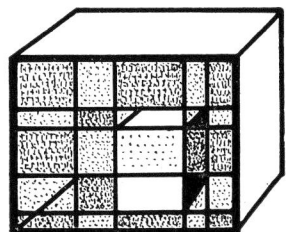

3. PATTERN AND SPACE

The Combination of Pattern with Pictorial Space

The integration of flat pattern with pictorial space is one of the most interesting, difficult, and important of the painter's problems. Since every painter discovers innumerable ways of doing this, for the problem will vary in each picture, you can understand that only *one* basic solution is demonstrated in the above diagrams.

The first diagram shows flat pattern; the second represents pictorial space. Both have been combined in the third diagram in such a way that pattern now affects space, and space also affects pattern, yet both can still be seen at the same time. There is an unexplainable mystery in any combination of pattern and space, for it is one of the living qualities of painting and is also one of the reasons why subject matter in painting is *not* as important as is sometimes supposed.

Line Directions in Pattern and Space

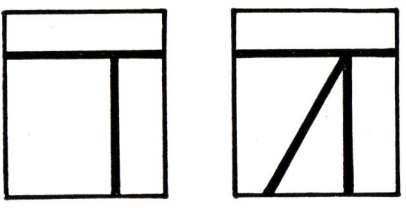

Vertical lines. Vertical lines will ordinarily lie on the surface of the picture plane as pattern, for they repeat two sides of the format. But in combination with a space-describing diagonal line, a vertical can then be seen *both* as pattern and as pictorial space.

Horizontal lines. Horizontal lines are usually pattern lines, for they also lie flat on the picture plane and repeat two format lines. But through relative positions, overlapping, and other means, horizontals can also help to describe space.

 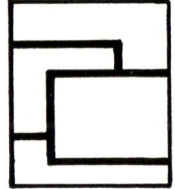

The diagonal. Most diagonals parallel to the picture plane will also act as pattern but, combined as converging lines, can also describe space. The diagonal in the first diagram can be seen as flat pattern, but in the second diagram this same diagonal has become half pattern and half pictorial space.

Opposed diagonals. (Not diagrammed.) The crossing of one line with another has a flattening effect. This crossing is also apt to appear static and create a strong focal point in pictures.

The triangle. A triangle can be made to appear either flat or deep. The triangle in the first diagram is flat, but in the second it can be seen *either* as flat pattern or as deep space.

 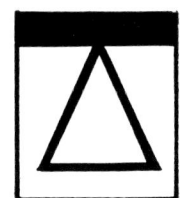

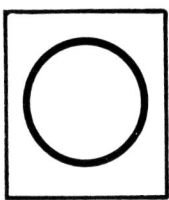 

The circle. A perfect circle does not describe space, but lies flat on the picture plane. An oval, however, can be made to describe space in pictures.

Curving lines. A curving line made from parts of a perfect circle will lie flat on the picture plane, but more freely drawn curves can be used to describe space.

The Importance of Color Values

The *value* of a color is simply its light or dark quality, in addition to its particular color. Pure yellow is always a light value; pure purple is always dark.

Value is of great importance to color in painting, for it is usually the dark and light *values* of color which help to define structure in pictures. This does not mean, however, that a correct *value* is enough, for the *color* of that value is of great importance as well.

The *placing* of values also affects adjacent color values, for a light color next to a dark will not only produce a strong contrast, but will apparently change the value and color of both.

All of the pictures in this book appear in *value*, which is, in one way, an asset, for to eliminate color from paintings can sometimes simplify explanation.

Functional Color in Painting

The over-all color effect in great painting is not usually the result of a predetermined color scheme (as in interior decoration), but develops out of the painter's struggle to combine pattern with space.

Color also has important spatial qualities such as the advancing effect of warm colors over cold. For instance, if equal areas of strong red and weak blue are placed side by side on the canvas, the red will apparently come forward, the blue recede. In other words, painters do not use colors for their intrinsic qualities as jewelers use the colors of jewels, but create what are apparently new colors by various combinations of colors, values, textures, areas, and shapes.

The Effect of Textures

Texture in painting can be actually rough or smooth, or textures can be simulated by brush strokes, spots, and so on.

Textures affect colors, the values of colors, and will heighten color differences. A consistent surface texture can also help to preserve the flatness of the picture plane.

Thought and Feeling

The foregoing has been a greatly simplified outline of some of the fundamentals of painting. You may now ask, "Do most painters know about these particular principles and do they use them in their work?" The answer is: yes and no. Many painters know how to create certain space-pattern effects while others who don't know also produce certain space-pattern effects. Instinct is essential to any painter—or call it feeling or emotion, as you will. But since an emotional state is unstable in any endeavor, it can safely be said that all painting is a combination of thought *and* feeling, with one or the other predominating at different times. This balance, of course, will vary with each painter. That is one of the reasons why painters seldom know at the beginning of a painting how it will finally develop. This is in direct contrast to the method of most advertising artists, who *render* an illustration with the end result foreseen from the start.

How to Look at the Pictures that Follow

At this point it might be well to turn to the beginning and read this section once again, for due to the necessity of presenting ideas one at a time, the earlier pages will then be better understood in relation to the pages that follow.

But in looking at paintings from now on, all of these isolated ideas should be combined into *one* concept—your own, for the *only* way to experience pictures is to *look* at pictures in your own way.

THE COMPARISON OF PAINTINGS WITH THEIR MOTIF PHOTOGRAPHS

The painters' statements beneath their paintings you will find in *italic type* so as not to confuse them with the author's words below.

ACME PHOTO

TIMES SQUARE · COLLECTION OF J. B. NEUMANN

Israel Litwak

Here at the beginning of the pictures is a naive-primitive painting. It is exceedingly rare to find a painting of this kind that has an actual motif, for most naive-primitive artists paint entirely from imaginative memory. No one *learns* to be a primitive, one *is;* and most primitive painters produce a painting on their first attempt—without previous painting experience.

Mr. Litwak, who is quite advanced in years, was asked why he had not painted the many electric signs that dominate Times Square. His answer (if not aesthetic) was direct and to the point. He simply said that no one had paid *him* to advertise.

Primitive or not, this picture has a great deal of charm, and although untrained, the artist has instinctively hit upon the fact that diagonal lines can be used to describe space in pictures.

PHOTOGRAPH BY G. V. GROVER FROM BLACK STAR

TIMES SQUARE · VAN DIEMEN-LILIENFELD

Frederick Franck

There could hardly be a greater contrast than exists between this painting and the naive-primitive picture you have just seen. Although both are pictorial statements of Times Square, and the naive-primitive painting exhibits a great deal of instinct and feeling, Frederick Franck's picture shows instinct and feeling *plus knowledge, experience, and skill.*

PHOTOGRAPH FROM FREDERICK FRANCK

CANNES · VAN DIEMEN-LILIENFELD

Frederick Franck

"First: What do I look for in nature? Why do I set up my easel here and not one hundred yards further on? I believe that I choose that which has interesting proportions of forms: sky, division of land and water, ships, etc. This is a primary, formal consideration. But a five-minute sketch will determine, confirm, or reject these proportions. And it may all be 'ideal' but the painting gets nowhere.

"Then I discover that this particular subject does not present the inexhaustible wealth of associations (for me) which I require at the moment.

"How often have we heard that the subject doesn't matter? *That is a half-truth. The subject does not matter in the finished painting.*"

Space has been increased in this painting by placing the distant buildings near the top of the canvas. This deep space has then been *decreased* by the shadow-like darks alongside the upper part of the pattern of masts in the foreground.

The diagonal directions of the yacht hulls also describe space which is again flattened by the vertical light reflections which fall across them.

PHOTOGRAPH BY HAL CHASE FROM BLACK STAR

BROOKLYN BRIDGE · KENNEDY

Stow Wengenroth

"Most of the really important ideas in the realm of picture-making find their beginnings in nature. It is the artist's temperament that finally selects the final subject of his picture from the infinite number of possibilities that nature affords.

"The selection is not too difficult—putting it into a strong and convincing form is the undertaking that presents the difficulties. Once the inspiration has been found, the artist must leave nature and depend on a skill and artistry quite removed from nature itself."

This lithograph by Stow Wengenroth is the first of three pictures by three artists who drew or painted from the same view of Brooklyn Bridge.

There is an unusual spatial device in this lithograph. The receding directions of the central cables also lie flat as a vertical line on the picture plane.

[39]

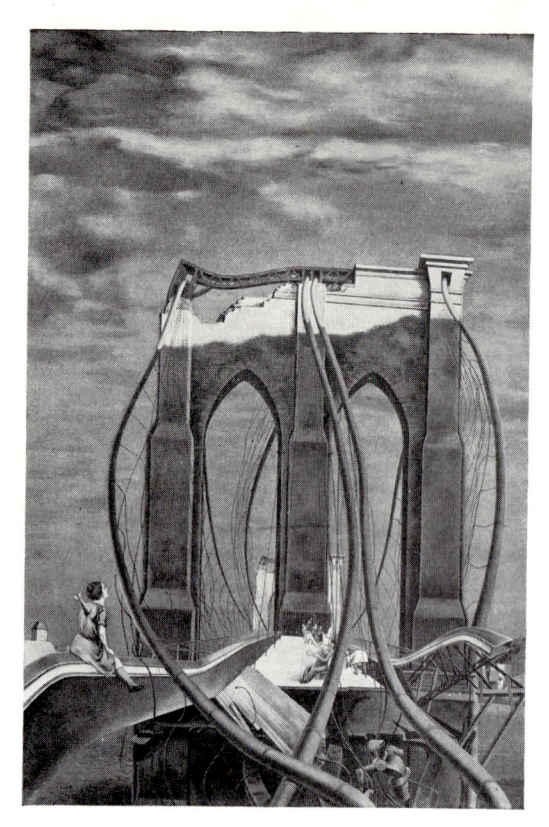

MENTAL GEOGRAPHY · DOWNTOWN

Louis Guglielmi

"The philosophical conception of 'Mental Geography,' to quote from an article of the day, '. . . painted during the Spanish Civil War. . . . I meant to say that an era had ended and that the rivers of Spain flowed to the Atlantic and mixed with our waters as well.'

"As is the case with other works that I produced at the time it was dubbed surrealism. Actually it anticipated the neo-romantic that was to become a popular vogue ten years later.

"Here the spatial idea was to fill up space and with the classic illusion of perspective rather than the formal creation of space. The glow of a setting sun on a doomed world, the small helpless figures all suggest a romantic melancholy."

Note how the rhythmic lines of the cables are used as contrast against the vertical directions on the bridge tower, and also how the horizontal cloud forms in space relate to the near and arbitrary light area above the two arches.

[40]

BROOKLYN BRIDGE · THE NEWARK MUSEUM, NEWARK, NEW JERSEY

Joseph Stella

"... for Brooklyn Bridge had become an ever-growing obsession ever since I had come to America...."

"Many nights I stood on the bridge—and in the middle alone—lost—a defenseless prey to the surrounding swarming darkness—crushed by the mountainous black impenetrability of the skyscrapers—here and there lights resembling suspended falls of astral bodies or fantastic splendors of remote rites—shaken by the underground tumult of the trains in perpetual motion, like the blood in the arteries—at times, ringing as alarm in a tempest, the shrill sulphurous voice of the trolley wires—now and then strange moanings of appeal from tugboats, guessed more than seen, through the infernal recesses below—I felt deeply moved, as if on the threshold of a new religion or in the presence of a new Divinity." [1]

[1] Reprinted from a monograph by Joseph Stella called *New York*, which contained the above painting of Brooklyn Bridge. This painting (1922) is one of many paintings by Joseph Stella of the same subject.

PHOTOGRAPH FROM HAZARD DURFEE

SKETCH FOR "SALT WATER FARM" · GRAND CENTRAL MODERNS

SALT WATER FARM · GRAND CENTRAL MODERNS

Hazard Durfee

"The architecture of a landscape and its mood are the two elements which are important to me. On our New England coast, these two elements are as much part of the quality of light as of the more concrete aspects of the landscape. This shifting light is of the sea; it is cool and hard, creating great distances and sharp focus. So, although the painting is built of patterns of light and shade, it is completely alien to the technique of French Impressionism which was created out of the soft feminine atmosphere of France. Also, as may be seen from the photograph and the paintings, I do not seek to recreate a scene, but rather, to make a picture from the elements of that scene which appeal to me."

Here are a motif photograph, a water-color sketch, and the finished oil painting. While both the sketch and painting use arbitrary space planes as part of their compositions, these planes are not used in the same way in both pictures.

[43]

PHOTOGRAPH BY THE AUTHOR

SKETCH FOR "14TH STREET ROOFTOP" · KENNEDY

Armin Landeck (1)

While the pictures by Armin Landeck on the next two pages are based on this charcoal sketch, each of the compositions was developed in a different way.

14TH STREET ROOFTOP · DRY POINT

Armin Landeck (2)

Here three definite light areas form a distinctive pattern in space which is only vaguely suggested in the motif photograph.

The pattern of windows on both the left and right sides of this dry point produce a staccato effect that also becomes part of pattern and space.

14TH STREET ROOFTOP · OIL · COLLECTION OF LYMAN BLOOMINGDALE

Armin Landeck (3)

"I can paint the average, more or less perfect egg from memory and at times enjoy the illusion that I have invented it, but I wouldn't care to paint a wrinkled egg without a model."

The tonal quality of this painting is in direct contrast to the sharper edges of the dry point opposite. Also, the ventilators on the rooftop have now become important in the composition, and the spatial thrust of the two skylights is used quite differently.

PHOTOGRAPHS BY THE AUTHOR

ROOFTOPS NO. 1 · DOWNTOWN

David Fredenthal (1)

"After I had returned to New York from a month in the deserts and mountains of New Mexico, the feeling of terrific compression of space in a large city motivated this picture. It is the first of twenty-five paintings from the same motif."

Five paintings from this series are shown on the next few pages. However, since the motifs for these pictures exist in all directions, it is impossible for the three photographs opposite to show all of the compositional elements found in all of the pictures.

FLIGHT OVER ROOFTOPS · WICHITA ART MUSEUM

David Fredenthal (2)

"An increased sense of compression and the imposing tactility of surfaces resulted in this painting, which was the eighth in this series."

SUMMER RAIN · DOWNTOWN

David Fredenthal (3)

"Having worked out the sense of compression to a degree, the lyric beauty of weather interested me, for the falling rain introduced new vertical relationships."

WIND AND SUN · DOWNTOWN

David Fredenthal (4)

"The wind and sun movements helped me in this picture to find gay new horizontal relationships."

The originals of the water colors shown on these two pages are only about eight by ten inches in size. The three preceding pictures, however, are somewhat larger.

STRIVING CITY · DOWNTOWN

David Fredenthal (5)

"This is the twenty-fifth in this series of pictures. By this time, my studio roof began to include all of New York City, its great rhythms, compressions, surges, vistas, and minute forms integrating into a statement so personal that I included a self-portrait.

"The dancing figures are not entirely imaginative, for there is a ballet company in the same building as my studio.

"I have worked on this series of paintings for over a year, and during that time I have watched the construction of one large building and the tearing down of another. Both are indicated in this final painting."

As this book goes to press, David Fredenthal has added three more paintings to this series.

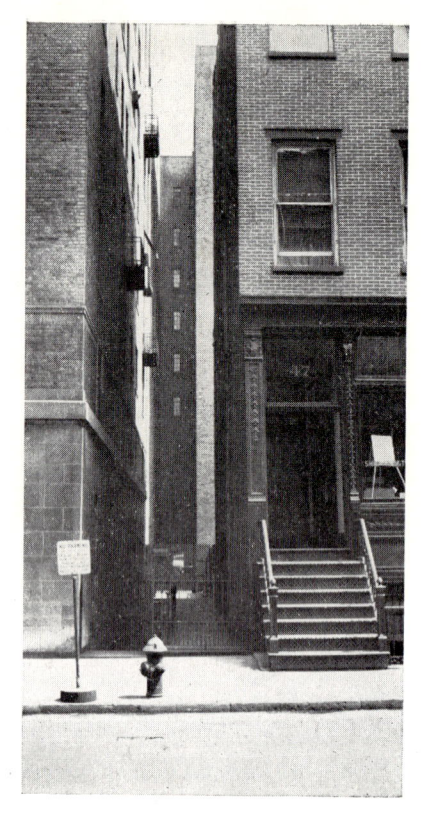

PHOTOGRAPH BY THE AUTHOR

GREENWICH VILLAGE PASSAGEWAY · LUYBER

Dorothy Andrews

"My pictures are based on many sketches done directly from nature. In them I try to make as simple and concise a statement as I am able about that particular aspect of nature which has affected me."

Space is suggested in this painting in a somewhat similar manner to the "exploded" cube diagram used earlier to help explain pictorial space. This effect you can see in the various planes of the passageway and also on the adjacent walls. Even the spatial relationships set up between the two railings act in a corresponding way.

PHOTOGRAPH FROM VICTOR ARNAUTOFF

CALIFORNIA LANDSCAPE

Victor Arnautoff

"I like to paint landscapes because nature is that dense medium in which man has to exist and in order to survive has to know it and utilize its unlimited richness for the benefit of the Human Race.

"I do not copy the landscape, nor do I twist it for the glory of the formula of plastic values, but I do generalize and adjust some parts in order to express in the given 'picture-fragment' the bigness of the whole."

Atmospheric perspective, where values become progressively lighter as they recede into space, is sometimes dangerous to use in landscape painting, for too much atmospheric perspective is apt to produce a "hole-in-the-wall" picture where interest is carried *back* without the possibility of return.

Victor Arnautoff has successfully overcome this effect (which is evident in the motif) by his use of strong darks in both the background and foreground planes. This arbitrary use of dark values helps to bring the background area into closer relationship with the flatness of the picture plane.

PHOTOGRAPH BY GEORGE L. LAWRENCE

FARM NEAR CHAUTAUQUA · LUYBER

Revington Arthur

"I have never had any urge to reproduce the appearance of nature, but often, some arrangement or some symbol in nature (i.e., the shape of a tree, a cloud, a patch of grass, a series of hills) will set off a 'chain reaction' of creative ideas which result in a painting. On first seeing this 'Chautauqua Farm,' I had an impulse to rearrange the farm buildings into an interesting design and to make it 'work' with the other shapes and forms around it. I ignored everything which was not absolutely necessary to the purpose of the composition, and with the shapes and forms which I did employ, I improvised, distorted and abstractly developed the 'whole' picture, often at the expense of actual resemblance to nature. By concentrating on only the essentials and their abstract organization, the result is often more 'true to nature' in feeling than a strict representation. In short, nature never dictates the painting, but often suggests it."

The large unifying triangle which integrates this water color can be seen either as extending back into space or as a flat pattern on the picture plane. Even the staccato pattern of small haystacks is part of both the space and pattern quality of this encompassing triangle. These haystacks, by the way, cannot be seen in the motif photograph, for they are from another part of the farm.

PHOTOGRAPH FROM MORRIS BLACKBURN

The technical quality of this particular motif photograph is unfortunately not of the best, for it was enlarged (like others you will see) from a section of a very small negative. This book, however, is not intended as a comparison of photography with painting as such. Photographs are used here only as substitutes for segments of the actual world.

RED SUMMER SUN · LUYBER

Morris Blackburn

"I use nature as a kind of sub-starting point. I do not imitate or try to improve on nature. I do try to improve on my own painting. Actually the canvas itself is the starting point. Each proportion or size of canvas has its own laws and is subject to a different and intuitive form of attack.

"A painting is the result of the quality of the act of painting—the structural integration of form and color, the emotional maturity of the painter himself and his ability to synthesize his vision, experience, and intuition.

"In short, I take the prerogative of the composer of music and obey no laws other than those inherent in the medium of painting."

Two themes are woven together in this painting where a variety of related dark shapes in space are integrated with a highly inventive pattern of reflected light. But these black and white values do not truly represent this picture's color, for the *red* sun in the actual painting is almost the same value as the gray sky—consequently causing a vibration not possible to show in value.

PHOTOGRAPH FROM AARON BOHROD

LANDSCAPE, SOUTHERN ILLINOIS

Aaron Bohrod

"In all my painting I have chosen to work only from the elements of and the basic arrangements I can see in nature; or, in combination with the works of man. This I do with a greater or lesser faithfulness to actual appearance as I may desire. Because of my usual satisfaction with the forms nature has created, my deviations usually take the form of rearrangement rather than that of radical distortion.

"I believe that only the constant refreshening that comes from a direct and humble approach to nature saves the artist from the inevitable sterility engendered by feeding constantly on his own trumped-up ideas, no matter how inventive or ingenious he may be." [1]

The fact that you can see all of the tree in the painting adds to its completeness, which can easily be realized by comparison with the motif photograph. The variety of textures also helps to unify the painting. The placing of the white horse and the figures animates the composition without their becoming focal points to retard rhythmic movement. It is characteristic of figures in almost any landscape painting to become much more important in the composition than would an inanimate object of the same size and color.

[1] Reprinted from *Pictures, Painters, and You*, by Ray Bethers. Pitman Publishing Corporation, 1948.

STILL LIFE WITH THE SPINET

Jean de Botton

"The subject of a picture is a politeness that the painter bestows on the spectator."

This still-life painting was the source of the formal organization in the painting "Les Courses à Longchamps—Paris," shown opposite.

There is a great deal to learn by comparing these two pictures, for similar dark and light shapes appear in similar positions in each. In other words, *two* pictures have been constructed on *one* basic composition.

LES COURSES À LONGCHAMPS—PARIS · KNOEDLER

Jean de Botton

"To my knowledge nothing better has ever been written on the subject of nature in art than by Delacroix who said: 'I consult nature as a dictionary.'

"Personally I go to nature for an analysis only—as a laboratory experiment.

"Creation is something else.

"Creation means synthesis.

"An artist cannot create by reproducing nature literally—no more than a playwright can realize a dialogue by listening through keyholes—a novelist write a novel by assembling facts and gossip, or a musician compose a sonata on the sea by recording the sounds of the waves.

"Art is a personal synthesis of nature."

PHOTOGRAPH FROM LOUIS BOUCHÉ

PONY RIDE · KRAUSHAAR

Louis Bouché

"Since I bought my country home, I have come to realize how superb is the work of nature. It makes you truly religious! Nature is the great artist. I have lived too long and painted too much to feel that painting is everything. Love and living are more important. If you love, you love beauty and therefore you love nature. Unfortunately many artists today get their biggest kick out of other people's art and don't go to the source of all great art—nature. Too much eclecticism inevitably leads to sterility." [1]

Pictorial space *behind* the picture plane has already been discussed and diagrammed, but *vertical* space possibilities have not been mentioned thus far.

This effect is demonstrated above where vertical space is described between the lamps on the two front poles and the figure of the boy with the spotted pony. This spatial feeling is also part of an implied line forming one side of a triangle.

[1] Reprinted from the *American Artist* magazine.

PHOTOGRAPH BY HANS NAMUTH

HICK'S ISLAND

Alexander Brook

"It is rarely that I have any interest in nature per se as subject matter. The human touch, things that man has made or that he or the elements have destroyed attract my attention. The valleys, mountains and deserts of the West with their color, drama and awesomeness mean nothing to me as painting motifs compared to the often depressing slovenliness of the South, the occasional humorous aspect or a combination of both. The accompanying illustration is a fish factory destroyed in the 1938 hurricane; I painted it just before man removed the roof of the only remaining house as the photograph shows and now has razed it entirely."

To call this particular motif unpromising would be an understatement, yet the painting is filled with pattern, space, and movement. There is an interesting subjective line (implied) from the log on the beach to the house on the left which reaches up to the white cloud and back again to the log. The placing of the sea gulls functions as a staccato pattern to animate an otherwise uninteresting area.

[69]

PHOTOGRAPH FROM NICOLAI CIKOVSKY

SHINNECOCK HILLS · ASSOCIATED AMERICAN ARTISTS

Nicolai Cikovsky

"I paint directly from nature and am guided in choice of subject chiefly by the lyrical and poetical. Color relation, contrast of structural design—boats, fishing houses, piers against sky, water, and trees—changes in sky and clouds, all have strong appeal. Spectacular and panoramic landscapes do not interest me, preferring as I do intimate subjects that I see and have contact with in everyday life—gardens, ponds, city squares, parks, and streets. Often I enliven landscapes with human figures, or if my interest at the time happens to be the decorative aspect of landscape, I combine it with still life."

This motif photograph appears only as a fragment of the actual world, with the angle of the road leading off the picture in both directions. The painting, however, is complete in itself and has a life of its own in consequence. The clouds and trees are not only descriptive, but act as space and pattern, with the various positions of the trees creating an elliptical space movement behind the picture plane.

Note how important the tree forms in the upper right become, for they break the long line of the horizon to prevent your attention from leaving the picture at that point. Notice also how the two darker trees add variety to all of the other trees.

PHOTOGRAPH FROM HOWARD COOK

RIO GRANDE · GRAND CENTRAL MODERNS

Howard Cook

"*Motif originating in life movement itself becomes a world of its own on canvas; color is used to illuminate the mood and to provide functional movement integrated with the design structure. In the Southwest to express the elemental qualities of this volcanic earth, formal organization dictated by essential character; paintings of the New York theme impressed with the beauty of ordered mass and vertical grace which are not dissimilar in spirit from the Southwest in their creative challenge.*"

No doubt the *actual* motif for this landscape presents a monumental effect, but this is not evident in the motif photograph.

This effect is very much in evidence in the painting, however, for every directional line and plane is so placed as to give this feeling.

There is also a definite spatial relationship between the curve of the river in the lower right and the flowing shapes of the two clouds in the sky. The fact that the plane of ranch houses and trees is at an angle to the horizontal lines of the format contributes to the feeling of movement in the picture.

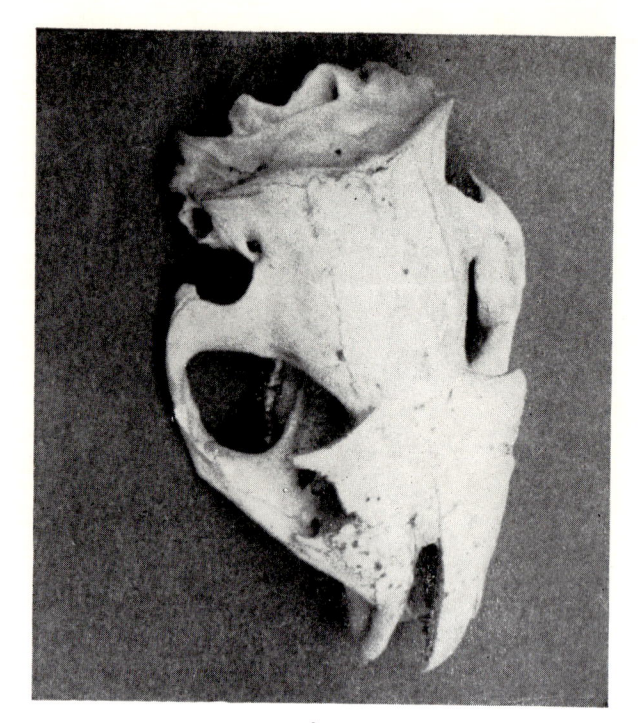

PHOTOGRAPH OF A WOODCHUCK'S SKULL FROM RUSSELL COWLES

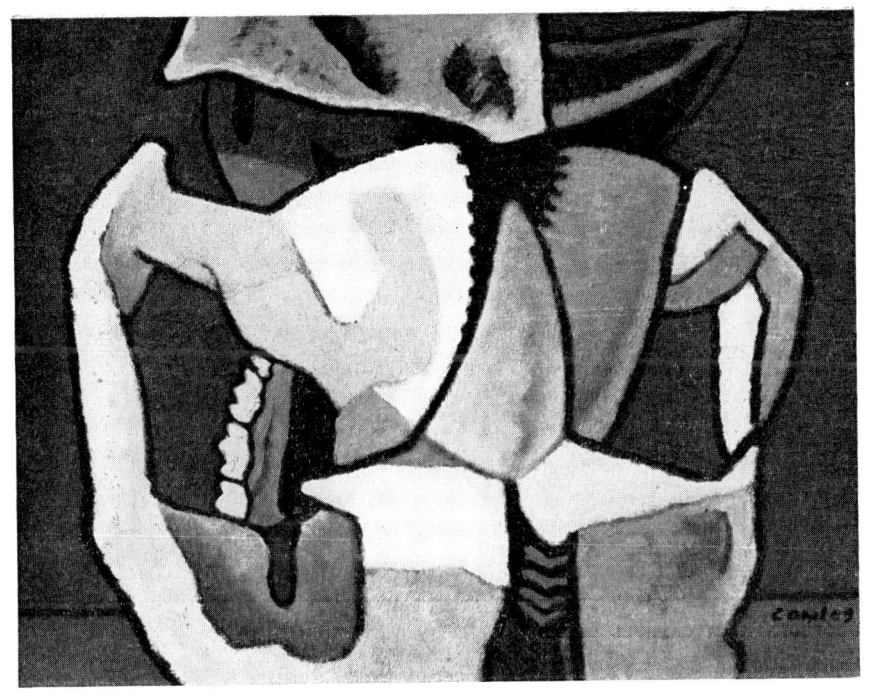

THE DICTATOR · KRAUSHAAR

Russell Cowles

"Nature is the artist's dictionary, to which he turns not just for facts, for information, but for countless sensory impressions. These sensory images are the source and stimulus of the creative imagination. Through the contemplation of nature the artist develops a sense of relation among things and among the parts of things. When a feeling of interesting and significant relations is incorporated in a painting the result is on the way to being a work of art."

You might not expect a woodchuck's skull to inspire a painting, but here it is. The painting, however, has departed entirely from any actual world meaning a woodchuck's skull might have and has become an emotionally felt organization of related shapes, colors, and textures on a flat inert plane.

There is a moral to this. Everything in the visible world has certain shapes, colors, and textures which are of intrinsic interest, aside from any part they may also have in identifying an object or in describing its use, association, or function.

PHOTOGRAPH BY CARROLL BURKE

FACTOR'S WALK · LUYBER

Lamar Dodd

"*I have felt, in my own work to date, that some contact with nature is absolutely essential. This does not necessarily mean that a direct relationship exists between the painting and the visual image of the natural object. The painter establishes any such relationship by abstracting [1] his material from his entire visual experience. By this means, paintings seem to grow structurally with natural objects acting as a suggestive factor.*"

Most painters look at (and sometimes paint) their pictures upside down. This is also a good way for anyone to look at creative paintings, for the abstract elements of the composition will then be more evident than the meaning of any particular subject matter.

This painting is a very good example on which to try this way of looking at pictures, for if you turn it upside down or sideways, its organization will not suffer in consequence.

The horizontal base line which parallels the overhead walk is also interesting, for it is both a space and pattern line.

---

[1] Lamar Dodd's use of the word "abstract" (while absolutely correct) has exactly the opposite meaning from that intended by the author elsewhere in this book.

PHOTOGRAPH FROM STEPHEN ETNIER

LATE AFTERNOON

Stephen Etnier

"I am stimulated by many aspects of nature, particularly the effects of light. In order to communicate my excitement, I paint directly from nature when possible, but where necessary reorganize and for emphasis simplify. This procedure seems essential in my endeavor to convey my responses to as many sympathetic people as I can. I do not, however, try to impose upon them the translation of abstract, esoteric, or self-initiated symbols."

The feeling of space in this painting has been greatly increased through raising the horizon line, and the arbitrary reversal of the curved road allows this new curve to become part of the elliptical space movement of the white-capped waves. Interest has also been concentrated *inside* the format by the complete elimination of the sky.

PHOTOGRAPH FROM DEAN FAUSETT

AUTUMN IN NEW ENGLAND · COLLECTION OF MRS. GERARD LAMBERT

Dean Fausett

"Often in nature the arrangement is a far more confused series of details than the eye is capable of appreciating simultaneously—sometimes these details prevent the important and meaningful portion of the subject from dominating—especially if the painter sets them down with equal importance.

"Visually speaking, the eye sees only what it is looking at immediately, other forms diffuse or soften when not in focus. Therefore it is often necessary to also diffuse or soften those edges, details and the like in a painting which are not of prime importance to the artist's esthetic concept.

Often the very forms must be changed, subdued, moulded, enlarged, detailed or simplified, in fact, changed in any way the artist feels will make the production his own private theater, more convincing and more satisfying."

Although at first glance this painting might seem to be fairly representational, it is actually filled with arbitrary deviations from nature. There is an accented spatial diagonal, for instance, from the middle left to the lower right. An angular hill has been added to help unify the central area, and the tree forms and clouds have been placed so as to be part of space and pattern.

PHOTOGRAPH BY OLIVER BAKER

LOW TIDE · GRAND CENTRAL MODERNS

Ruth Gikow

The dominant horizontal directions in the motif have been transformed into a series of thrusts leading through a somewhat elliptical movement. This movement is contained in parts of both the background and foreground, but is given variety by the use of several diagonal lines.

There is also a definite spatial relationship between the rock at the right and the diagonal piling on the left that is partially suggested in the motif photograph.

PHOTOGRAPH BY THE AUTHOR

OBSOLETE STRUCTURE · DOWNTOWN

Louis Guglielmi

"In 'Obsolete Structure' I have transformed the original three-dimensional objects onto a purely two-dimensional picture plane. These shapes and spaces have been organized in a kinetic and imaginative manner. The 'words and music' in this painting are in direct contrast to 'Mental Geography' on page 40.

" 'Obsolete Structure' is in the language of the painter rather than that of the man of letters."

The rhythmic composition of this painting makes the motif look very incomplete. You can see how the placing of the iceman and his truck hold attention to the foreground plane which would otherwise be lost in an illusion of distance. Also, the motif's strong diagonal direction is counteracted by the reversed continuation of the stairway forms in the upper part of the painting.

PHOTOGRAPH FROM JOHN HALEY

PENITENTE COUNTRY · MORTIMER LEVITT

John Haley

"In approaching a painting I try to find what is likely to be there. This does not mean that I am at a loss as to what to expect. That which evolves is always a surprise. What I hope for is some of the flow and change and continuous realignment of space groups on the painted surface that characterizes what seems to me to be the underlying relation of forms in art and in nature."

Space has been integrated to the picture plane in this painting partly through the use of an inventive pattern of heavy outlines, similar in its flattening effect to the leaded outlines in stained-glass windows. Notice also how the picket fences, the crosses on the ground, and the cross on the steeple are related and function both as pattern and as space.

PHOTOGRAPH FROM ERIC ISENBURGER

ROMAN WALLS · KNOEDLER

Eric Isenburger

"In my painting of the 'Roman Walls' I have tried to express my impressions of Rome. Walking along the old Appian Road you find ancient Rome in all its magnitude. These very walls I painted are humble walls not at all of the great past. But for some reason they became the essence of the strongly melancholic mood I always experienced on my walks through Rome."

    The converging lines in the motif force attention to the right and consequently out of the photograph. This has been overcome in the painting by making the wall parallel to the picture plane, by flattening the curve of the curbstone, and by unifying the various dark shapes to form an elliptical pattern in space. The white areas are also related to one another in a similar way.

PHOTOGRAPH BY GEORGE KARFIOL

THE COVE

Bernard Karfiol

"I've studied 'The Cove,' which is here reproduced, and in translating onto canvas have tried to intensify all that I felt in color, form, and spirit. The visual world is paintable always and everywhere. The more one listens, watches, and grows, the more secrets nature gives up. Even the commonest weeds suggest beautiful shapes and color."

Space is greatly reduced in the motif photograph where the horizon and the top edge of the rocks are described by the same horizontal line. This has been clarified in the painting where the horizon is above the rock formation.

Space in pictures is best described when *up* means *back* on the picture plane. This means that recession into space is seen from above, as in everyday experience we normally see space in front of us when we look down.

This does not mean that space seen from below (clouds in space, for instance) is difficult to indicate but only that space as seen from above is usually easiest to understand in pictures.

PHOTOGRAPH FROM KARL KASTEN

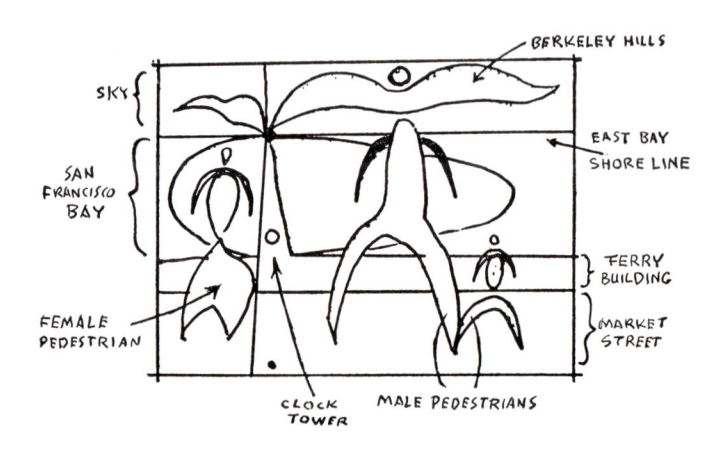

THE EMBARCADERO · COLLECTION OF MISS HAZEL HENSEN

Karl Kasten

"*In selecting a landscape motif for a painting I look for that aspect of the subject which best presents its 'essential' qualities; for example, if the subject were a bridge, I would select that view which expresses 'bridgeness' most effectively. On the basis of sketches made on the scene, I begin the painting in my studio. As I proceed with the painting, the original sketches are put aside and the identity of the motif is sacrificed to the development of plastic values. Finally, when the painting has come into being, the motif which inspired it may be quite difficult to discern, the relationship of space, color, line, etc., having become paramount.*"

    This painting comes very close to being a pure abstraction (without recognizable subject matter), yet, as you can see, it derives from Market Street in San Francisco.

    Karl Kasten has drawn the diagram on the opposite page to help identify the beginnings of the abstract shapes which developed during the painting of the picture.

PHOTOGRAPH BY THE AUTHOR

CITY HALL IN WHITE · MIDTOWN

Dong Kingman

"The old against the new, the complex against the simple, yin against yang, like and dislike, are the things I want to say in my pictures. I paint as I see, but also as I think." [1]

The motif, as you can see, is filled with empty and non-functioning areas with little interest within these accidental shapes. But among many other devices, the great variety of textures in the painting helps to make all parts of the picture functional. Note also how Dong Kingman has changed the *position* of many forms, to help unify his picture.

[1] Reprinted from *Pictures, Painters, and You*, by Ray Bethers. Pitman Publishing Corporation, 1948.

PHOTOGRAPH FROM GEORGINA KLITGAARD

ARBOR DAY AT THE SCHOOL · REHN

Georgina Klitgaard

"In this motif two basic forms predominate, the crescent arch of the blooming bough, and the vertical of tree, house and tower. Repetitions of the curve and the vertical are found in the structural lines of the landscape.

"These forms are not arbitrary, but are an interpretation of nature's unity and emphasis. They are universal and supply the basic structure which a cross-section of nature lacks, but which nature possesses as a whole."

Here is an excellent example of the use of planes which become part of this picture's movement and also relate objects in varying positions in space. Note how the diagonal on the right binds the foreground, roof, trees, hills, and sky as they all move back into space. This diagonal would be too insistent, however, if its dominant direction was not turned by the curving directions on the left-hand side.

PHOTOGRAPH BY PATRICK

TIDE WASH · ROSENBERG

Karl Knaths

"*Contact with nature may be essential for the painter. It does not necessarily mean to copy from the data of the natural eye. Even where the pictorial means have been tortured into duplicating the resemblance of natural surfaces, the esthetic value lies in the hidden plastic synthesis. Not to go from nature to the canvas, but from the canvas to nature and to be objective in pictorial terms. To make music as Apollo gave the term. So to be expressive and communicate something of beauty, which the poet says, is a joy forever.*"

There is a strong diagonal direction on the left which unites all planes from near to far, and which returns to the picture plane at the extreme right.

A variety of inventive textures also play an important part in the space and pattern relationships.

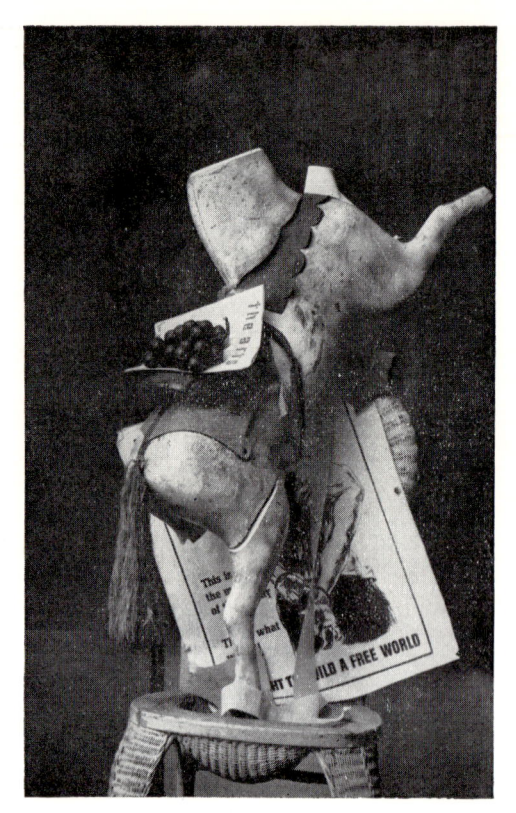

PHOTOGRAPH BY COLTEN

HEADLESS HORSE WHO WANTS TO JUMP · DOWNTOWN

Yasuo Kuniyoshi

"For me, reality is a starting point and at the same time a point of departure. Feeling, imagination and intuition mingled with reality create more than actuality, evoke an inner meaning indicative of one's experience, time, circumstance and environment. This is reality."

At first glance the form and textures of the motif may appear to have been quite accurately followed, but on second glance you will see that this is not so. Aside from the reorganization of form, every brush stroke has been applied as only Kuniyoshi knows how. In addition to individual attitudes toward composing pictures, the consistent character of brush strokes can help a great deal in unifying pictures.

PHOTOGRAPH BY THE AUTHOR

FOG—BOWLING GREEN · SALPETER

Irving Lehman

"*I believe that through abstract art one can experience the tensions and mobility of our times deeply. Through color, line, and rhythmic mobile units of form, I strive to recreate the tensions in a given scene into an aesthetic order. The release from the necessity to relate each form and color to the static momentary vision gives wings to one's imagination. Creation then proceeds, I feel, to whatever heights the struggles of our age can stir it.*"

The drifting wisps of fog have here been converted into transparent forms which fluctuate between deep space and the picture plane as part of an over-all geometric organization.

Transparency in painting allows one to "see through" otherwise opaque forms and in consequence to feel various spatial positions at the same time. These fluctuating planes are part of the pattern-space combination, at the same time creating an air of mystery.

PHOTOGRAPH BY THE AUTHOR

THE BRIDGE · CONTEMPORARY ARTS

John Chapman Lewis

"The composition of 'The Bridge' was worked out in my studio from sketches made at the location, eliminating that which I felt irrelevant to the finished painting. I sought to retain the basic shapes presented by the street and ramps leading onto the bridge, the compact group of buildings in the right-hand section, and the bridge itself. The color scheme was kept simple, allowing for greater freedom in the handling of textures."

The elliptical movement in and out of space in this painting is very evident, especially when compared to the lack of unity in the motif. The painting is also unified by consistent textures over the entire canvas and by relationships of thrusting and rhythmic directional lines.

PHOTOGRAPH BY MILDRED TOLBERT

THE VALLEY BELOW · LUYBER

Ward Lockwood

"A year after making this painting I find myself comparing it to the photograph of the motif made a few days ago. I see that the 'patch-work' fields occupy relatively a much greater surface area in the painting—mountains and sky seem to be more literally interpreted. Often what strongly strikes the emotions of a painter will be instinctively exaggerated in size, color or form."

The rectangular planes in the sky are directly related to the rectangular fields, to give an over-all feeling of pattern and space. There is also an elliptical space movement through the angular and directional relationships of houses, fields, mountains, and sky.

PHOTOGRAPH FROM ERLE LORAN

ROCK EQUILIBRIUM

Erle Loran

"*Nature remains the primary source for man's ideas and speculations in both art and science. Since man is one of the tiny products of nature he can hardly expect to become free of her. It would be difficult to demonstrate that any art had been produced that bears no debt to nature in some facet or other. For me the ever-changing aspect of the outside world continues to provide ideas for painting, but the original subject is rarely more than a generating source. What counts is the invention, fantasy, and artistic structure that may be organically developed from a set of forms observed in nature.*"

I first knew Erle Loran in 1940, when he was working on his book, *Cezanne's Composition*, published by the University of California Press. Today, *Cezanne's Composition* is still in great demand and has become the standard work on the subject.

My own book owes a great deal to Erle Loran, for to the best of my knowledge, he was the first to use motif photographs to help clarify composition in pictures; and although he took most of the motif photographs which appear in *his* book, this is the first time a painting by Erle Loran has appeared with its matching motif photograph.

PHOTOGRAPH FROM LUIGI LUCIONI

THE THREE GRACES

Luigi Lucioni

"At this moment I am not quite sure who said that Art is holding up one's mirror to Nature. Whoever said it, I am sure did not mean it literally, unless one takes into consideration that 'one's mirror' may be symbolic. Each one sees nature differently and therefore it is possible that 'one's mirror' should show results as different as abstract design and my own particular viewpoint. People have often said that I was 'photographic'; some have meant it as a great compliment, others as a scornful insult, so again it depends on one's own meanings. Nature to me is an inspiration and I have the greatest respect and awe of it, but I feel that in studying nature for art one does not necessarily copy it. The palette is a very limited substitute for the manifold attributes of nature, therefore I feel that I want to interpret nature with the limitations of the palette; consequently a great deal of careful simplification goes into every painting that I do, be it a landscape, a portrait, or a still life."

Some of the solidity of Luigi Lucioni's water color is achieved by the countless variety of textures on almost all planes of space. This quality will be more evident when compared to the soft values in the photograph, which progressively lighten as they recede.

PHOTOGRAPH BY THE AUTHOR

LIGHT AND SHADE UNDER THE EL · FEIGL

Nan Lurie

"*Discussion of aesthetic theory, it seems to me, deals with elements in isolation that do not* EXIST *in isolation. Since painting is a visual experience, like a bird in flight, it cannot be frozen into words.*

"*The process of interweaving forms and cross-currents of motion seems to me much like counterpoint in music. When one eliminates the human figure from a scene, ordinarily passive elements—a shadow, a door, a traffic sign—become dominant. The inanimate is dramatized. Psychology is part of the scene. Painting today, I believe, includes emotion as one of its formal plastic elements.*"

The dead area you can see in the lower left of the motif photograph has been given meaning in the painting partly through the inventive placing of the directional traffic signs. Notice also in the painting how the scumbled texture in the sky not only adds interest as surface quality, but also limits the effect of space.

[113]

PHOTOGRAPH BY THE AUTHOR

WOOLWORTH BUILDING, NEW YORK, NO. 3
STIEGLITZ COLLECTION, METROPOLITAN MUSEUM OF ART

John Marin

"So to begin—is the life of a great city confined only to the people and animals on its streets and in its buildings? Are the buildings themselves dead? We have been told somewhere that a work of art is a thing alive—you cannot make a work of art from having beheld that which responds not to that which is within you—therefore if these buildings move one they too must have life so that the whole city is also alive, so that buildings, people and all are alive—the more they move me the more are they alive for me." [1]

John Marin's etching was made thirty-five years before this motif photograph was taken, yet there is still a certain relationship between the etching and the motif as it now appears.

[1] Reprinted with the permission of John Marin, and Alfred Stieglitz Archives, Collection of American Literature, Yale University Library, New Haven, Connecticut.

[115]

PHOTOGRAPH BY DR. GEORGE FULLER

TREES, SEA AND ROCKS

Jose Moya del Pino

"The visual and emotional impact of the motif is always the source in my approach to painting. A too-close rendition of the subject fails to echo my sensations; so through a process of designing, addition and subtraction—but mostly through elimination—I come nearer to registering my emotions before nature.

"Like some other painters on the Pacific coast, I have felt the influence of classic Chinese painting in my attitude toward pictorial expression, thus, to recreate rather than to represent is my aim."

Deep space has been indicated both by the high horizon and by the relative placing of the points of land on each side as they step *up* and consequently back in the composition.

The single tree as shown in the motif photograph served as a "model" for all three trees as they now appear in the painting.

PHOTOGRAPH BY THE AUTHOR

RANCHOS CHURCH · STIEGLITZ COLLECTION, METROPOLITAN MUSEUM OF ART

Georgia O'Keeffe

"*If my painting is what I have to give back to the world for what the world gives to me, I may say that these paintings are what I have to give at present....*

"*What I have been able to put into form seems infinitesimal compared with the variety of experience.*" [1]

There is definite movement and weight within the interlocking masses of this painting, as well as a feeling of radiation from a mysterious central point in space.

[1] From a catalogue of one of **Georgia O'Keeffe's** exhibitions.

PHOTOGRAPH BY THE AUTHOR

NOCTURNE · COLLECTION OF MR. AND MRS. SEYMOUR SCHUMAN

Arthur Osver

"Yes, my painting derives from nature. It is no accident that I live in a large city—the things I paint are found there. The ability to deal directly with my subject results in an ever-growing awareness of its possibilities. And that's the big thing. For I feel very strongly that it is only through such a living, energetic contact with nature that I can realize whatever happens to be unique and personal in my work."

This motif photograph shows a rooftop, some walls, a few pipes, and several buildings in the distance. As a picture, it means no more than that, and most of these objects are also shown in the painting.

Why, then, is the painting a more complete statement than the photograph? I think it is mainly a matter of relationships, and although the entire picture demonstrates this, the reversal of the laws of perspective in the building on the extreme right is one of the qualities which unifies the picture. For rather than being purely descriptive, this building has also been considered as a *plane direction* in relation to every other element in the picture.

PHOTOGRAPH FROM ROBERT PHILIPP

GLOUCESTER HARBOR · COLLECTION OF MARCEL STIEGLITZ

Robert Philipp

"*I find landscape painting very relaxing as I turn to it from figure painting. The first thing that happens to me when I regard the piece of landscape which shall be the subject of my picture is that its mood captures me and holds me spellbound.*

"*My receptive attitude towards nature does not impel me to try to reproduce it at all. I interpret and transpose it. My reactions to the currents of color in tonal atmosphere, the plastic relationships in the composition are my motivating impulses as I feverishly paint my picture to completion.*"

The curve of the passageway leading to the building on the rock has been greatly accented in the painting to form part of the *movement* in the picture, as a flowing line in contrast to the static effect of the distant horizontal line.

Notice, also, how important the position of the fishing boat becomes in relation to the verticals of the flagpole and the structure on the rock.

PHOTOGRAPH FROM WALDO PEIRCE

BACK YARD · MIDTOWN

Waldo Peirce

"I think artists do better trying to express themselves in paint than by writing.

"There are a lot of things in nature which are pleasing enough, but which do not appeal as the makings of a painting. The painter looks on this or that manifestation of nature as something that appeals to him as a motif, not the literal anecdote, etc. What happens to the original nature doesn't matter at all—it is what happens on the canvas that is important."

The fragmentary effect of the motif photograph is intensified by the way the washing continues out of the picture at the left, and by the strong contrast of directional lines where the two trees extend out of the top.

Both of these faults have been eliminated in the painting, where the figures also rhythmically relate to the clothes on the line and to the entire picture.

PHOTOGRAPH BY THE AUTHOR

CITY SUNSET · REHN

Steve Raffo

"My interest is in people and the places in which they live; in the interplay of man and the world, used symbolically to express states of emotion. New York City is to me a particularly intense and varied extension of man's personality.

"In the painting 'City Sunset' I was concerned with movement, sunlight and youth entrapped by the City. Thus, the youth throwing a ball into space, caught in a shaft of sunlight enclosed by buildings—with the formal or abstract design stressing the thing expressed."

The lights and shadows in this painting are convincing from the standpoint of probability, yet they also form an abstract pattern of *light* and *dark* shapes which help to organize the picture.

PHOTOGRAPH FROM ZOLTAN SEPESHY

MORNING · MIDTOWN

Zoltan Sepeshy

"The artist is a product of nature. So are the materials with which he works —his paints and brushes—his organic equipment and his ideas. Naturalism in art is not rigid representation. No artist paints everything 'out there.' Not only would that be redundant duplication but it would take forever. The artist would be like Tristram Shandy who—writing the history of his life— took a year to write each day. No painting could incorporate all impressions indiscriminately.

"Art is selection and creation. It transfers—not imitates—what nature offers. It may seek abstract elements or fleeting impressions. Yet nature is the matrix from which it derives.

"There are no 'isms' except as pedants see them in retrospect. The artist can perhaps escape nature into an 'ism'—but then he is no longer an artist."

This painting is remarkable for its fidelity to the motif while at the same time departing from it.

Horizontal and vertical lines form part of the pattern on the picture plane, while the diagonal directions show movement into space. Notice, also, how important the curving back of the chair on the left becomes in counteracting the thrust of the diagonal line behind.

PHOTOGRAPH FROM BENTON SPRUANCE

WINTER MOONLIGHT · COLLECTION OF DR. AND MRS. FRANCIS HEED ADLER

Benton Spruance

"I find nature to be the most profound and varied vocabulary. From the texture of a leaf—a piece of bark—to the plane of water and man on earth —and finally to the reality of space—and of form and light in space—it returns to me the material out of which my pictures are made. Material to be ordered and contained on a surface; not copied but created as part of the surface—which may in turn reveal that form and space in a higher order."

    The direction of the stairs on the right is in close rhythmic relationship to the arbitrary plane above the church steeple, both becoming part of the spatial movement. Without these arbitrary planes, the repeated verticals of the church, buildings, and telegraph pole would be too static, preventing any suggestion of movement.

    These arbitrary planes can be felt as part of deep space and also as lying flat on the picture plane.

PHOTOGRAPH FROM REUBEN TAM

NORTHERN TERRAIN · DOWNTOWN

Reuben Tam

"*I do not paint directly from nature, but from experience and memory, and only when there is a persistence within me of the mood of a place. In each painting I seek a special, inevitable combination of the perceivable geological world of order and wilderness, and the inner, emotional world of memory, anticipation and identification. My aim is not to represent, nor to interpret nature; I paint to embody the spirit of place and thus make objective those poetic conditions, portents and possibilities of nature that move me deeply, personally, and hauntingly.*"

Here the geometric rock formations have been integrated with the more fluid forms of a surging sea, which helps to unify the foreground and background planes.

These planes appear closer together in this black-and-white reproduction, however, than they do in the full color of the actual painting.

PHOTOGRAPH FROM JOHN TAYLOR

THE TOWER

John Taylor

"The photo may not seem very relevant, but you may pick out some of the detail material. It is my practice 'on location' to make detailed drawings of the terrain that interests me, with a wide picture plane (about 13 x 19 inches) in pencil or conte crayon. It is from these that I develop compositional ideas, imaginatively and by transposition, in a series of small pen and ink drawings. It is from these latter that the picture itself develops."

This motif photograph and painting cannot be compared in the same way as most of the others, for only the *detail* came from the motif. As John Taylor says, the construction of the picture was evolved later. This construction is based on a strong horizontal direction broken by the vertical tower, with a staccato use of smaller elements organized on various planes in space.

[135]

PHOTOGRAPH FROM GLENN WESSELS

OREGON COAST

Glenn Wessels

"Nature for me is the source and essence of life. Part of it expresses itself as the world which we are, in which we are and which we see and feel. As a painter, I try to give symbolic life to my painting and hence I follow the principles of creation as I understand them, but since every form of matter has its own kind of life and limitation—the painter's medium amongst them—I try to interpret, not to copy nature.

While this motif photograph shows an interesting stretch of seacoast, the photograph itself is fragmentary and divided diagonally into two unequal parts.

This division you will not find in the painting, where arbitrary planes give unity to the entire picture. The strong diagonal feeling is also lessened by a variety of smaller directions which are repeated in the log pattern on the beach and in the geometric pattern of waves.

I must here acknowledge a great debt to my friend Glenn Wessels, for it was he who long ago pointed out a way of thinking which is reflected not only in this book, but in my other books as well.

[137]

PHOTOGRAPH FROM SOL WILSON

CHURCH ACROSS THE BAY · BABCOCK

Sol Wilson

"The motifs for my paintings I find wherever I live and they are those that I am constantly surrounded by. These motifs give me the initial push, the stimulus for a painting, after which I let my imagination work unhampered by the naturalistic exactness of, or fidelity to the original scene. Color and shapes are changed or created in accordance with the needs of the particular painting, however, not forgetting the character of the subject."

Every directional line in the motif photograph seems to concentrate interest on the left side, where nothing of particular interest occurs.

This has been overcome in the painting by controlled directions, where the placing of the piling, for instance, becomes very important both in filling an otherwise empty space and in directing interest to the background church. This implied direction then returns to the picture plane through the thrust of the wharf as part of a rotary movement in space which can be followed in either direction.

PHOTOGRAPH BY THE AUTHOR

BRIDGE · DOWNTOWN

Karl Zerbe

The similarity between this motif photograph and the painting is all the more striking from the fact that both are yet so different.

Two examples of this difference are found in the rhythmically organized pattern of the light and dark buildings in the painting, and in the unifying consistency of texture over the painting's entire area.

Pure Abstraction (Non-Objective) Painting

The painting on the opposite page does not and could not have a motif photograph. It is placed last because it is a *pure abstraction* (non-objective) and does not derive from specific forms in the actual world. In other words, a pure abstraction has no *subject matter* but must evoke emotion from the way certain lines, shapes, and directions are organized in space.

Few painters of pure abstractions, however, have always painted in this way, for almost all have painted from nature at some time at the beginning of their career.

LINE VARIATIONS NO. 1 · JANIS

Jean Xceron

"The highlight of the painting is not what it represents, but the way things in the picture are put together. In non-representational art we must not expect to see any natural objects such as we are accustomed to see in figurative painting. The pictorial elements, form, color, and space relationship, in this new approach to painting produce an 'object' which is not similar to a 'particular object' in naturalistic art, but exists and has its own life, nevertheless. This new 'objective' painting is called 'non-objective'."

All Pictures Are Not for All People

Some of the paintings in this book you may have liked very much, others you may not have liked at all. That is as it should be, for in either case you have exercised your judgment and expressed your feelings in a positive way. How much better to be positive rather than indifferent. Yet as you look at more and more pictures, your likes and dislikes cannot help but change.

Art is an endless road which branches out in many directions with new adventures all along the way. As you now look back, I hope you will remember that this book began with the idea that art is *not* a copy of nature and that paintings, as works of art, convey emotion rather than information.

The motif photographs were intended to represent certain factual information taken from the actual world. But because they are of necessity two-dimensional and confined to various formats, they are *not* nature but are already a step removed. Nor were they meant to move you emotionally as some of the paintings cannot help but do.

I'm sure that most of the painters intended their words to be primarily informational, but being artists, they cannot eliminate emotion from their point of view. But is not a point of view in itself emotional?

As for the author's words, they were designed to be as factual and unemotional as possible, to help you to understand better the basic *structure* and *limitation* of painting as an art form.

Your own reactions to these motif photographs, paintings, artists' words, and author's explanations should now be merged into your own experience, to be creatively applied as you either *paint* or *look* at pictures. If you are not a painter, one of the best ways to understand pictures is to paint them yourself, for Sunday painters are the most fortunate of all. Or perhaps you will wish to own certain paintings that "speak" to you. Some paintings cost very little and you may not have realized that many of the paintings shown in this book may still be for sale, for while it is true that painters enjoy *painting* pictures, they like to *sell* pictures as well.

> "An artist is not a man who gives the public what it wants: he is a man who makes the public want what he gives it."
> —ST. JOHN ERVINE

INDEX

Abstraction, 74-75
  Arthur on, 59
  defined, 17
  degrees of, 17
  Dodd on, 77
  Kasten on, 93
  Lehman on, 103
  pure, 17, 142, 143
  Xceron on, 143
Arbor Day at the School, Georgina Klitgaard, 97
Adler, Dr. and Mrs. Francis Heed, Collection, 131
Aesthetic experience, 15
AMERICAN ARTIST, 67
Andrews, Dorothy, 55
Arnautoff, Victor, 56, 57
Arrangement, 24
Arthur, Revington, 59
Associated American Artists, 71
Autumn in New England, Dean Fausett, 81

Babcock Galleries, 139
Back Yard, Waldo Peirce, 125
Baker, Oliver, photograph, 82
Blackburn, Morris, 60, 61
Bloomingdale, Lyman, Collection, 47
Bohrod, Aaron, 62, 63
Botton, Jean de, 64, 65
Bouché, Louis, 66, 67
Bridge, Karl Zerbe, 141
Bridge, The, John Chapman Lewis, 105
Brook, Alexander, 69
Brooklyn Bridge, Joseph Stella, 41
Brooklyn Bridge, Stow Wengenroth, 39
Burke, Carroll, photograph, 76

California Landscape, Victor Arnautoff, 57
CEZANNE'S COMPOSITION, Erle Loran, 109
Chase, Hal, photograph, 36
Church across the Bay, Sol Wilson, 139
Cikovsky, Nicolai, 70, 71
Circle, completeness of, 21
City Hall in White, Dong Kingman, 95

City Sunset, Steve Raffo, 127
Color, 28
Colten, photograph, 100
Communication, art as, 15
Completeness, 63, 71
  of circle, 21
Composition, 24, 77
COMPOSITION IN PICTURES, Bethers, 9
Conflict, opposed diagonals and, 21
Contemporary Arts, 105
Cook, Howard, 72, 73
Courses à Longchamps—Paris, Les, Jean de Botton, 64, 65
Cove, The, Bernard Karfiol, 91
Cowles, Russell, 74, 75
Curves, in pattern and space, 27
  as sadness, 21

Diagonals, falling character, 21
  opposed, 21
  in pattern and space, 26
Dictator, The, Cowles, 75
Dignity, verticals and, 21
Directions, line, 20
Dodd, Lamar, 77
Downtown Gallery, 40, 49, 51, 52, 53, 85, 101, 133, 141
Durfee, Hazard, 42, 43

Embarcadero, The, Karl Kasten, 92
Emotion, 17
  art and, 13, 14
  Lockwood on, 107
  symbols, 20
Etnier, Stephen, 78, 79
Ervine, St. John, 145

Factor's Walk, Lamar Dodd, 77
Farm near Chautauqua, Revington Arthur, 59
Fausett, Dean, 80, 81
Feeling, 17, 28
Feigl Gallery, 113
Flight over Rooftops, David Fredenthal, 50
Fog—Bowling Green, Irving Lehman, 103

[147]

Format, 20
14th Street Rooftop, Armin Landeck, in oil, 47
 in dry point, 46
 sketch for, 45
Frame, 20
Franck, Frederick, 35-37
Fredenthal, David, 49-53
FROM EYE TO CAMERA, Bethers, 9
Fuller, George, photograph, 116

Gikow, Ruth, 83
Gloucester Harbor, Robert Philipp, 123
Grand Central Moderns, 41, 42, 73, 83
Greenwich Village Passageway, Dorothy Andrews, 55
Grover, G. V., photograph, 34
Guglielmi, Louis, 40, 85

Haley, John, 86, 87
Headless Horse Who Wants to Jump, Yasuo Kuniyoshi, 101
Hick's Island, Alexander Brook, 69
Horizons, pictorial space and, 91
Horizontals, in pattern and space, 26
 quiet and restful, 21
 speed and, 21

Imagination in painting, 15
Information, art and, 13
Instinct, 29
Isenburger, Eric, 88, 89

Janis, Sydney, Galleries, 143

Karfiol, Bernard, 90
Karfiol, George, photograph, 90
Kasten, Karl, 92, 93
Kennedy Galleries, 39, 45
Kingman, Dong, 95
Klitgaard, Georgina, 96, 97
Knaths, Karl, 9, 99
Knoedler Art Galleries, 65, 89
Kuniyoshi, Yasuo, 101

Lambert, Mr. and Mrs. Gerard, Collection, 81
Landeck, Armin, 45, 46, 47
Landscape, Southern Illinois, Aaron Bohrod, 63
Late Afternoon, Stephen Etnier, 79
Lawrence, George L., photograph, 58
Lehman, Irving, 103
Lewis, John Chapman, 105
Levitt, Mortimer, Gallery, 87
Lhote, André, quoted, 12

Light and Shade under the El, Nan Lurie, 113
Line, subjective, 67, 69
Line directions, emotional effects, 20
 in pattern and space, 26
Line Variations No. 1, Jean Xceron, 143
Literature, time in, 19
Litwak, Israel, 33
Lockwood, Ward, 107
Loran, Erle, 108, 109
Low Tide, Ruth Gikow, 83
Lucioni, Luigi, 110, 111
Lurie, Nan, 113
Luyber, Joseph, Galleries, 55, 59, 61, 77, 107

Marin, John, 115
Matisse, Henri, on seeing, 15
Mental Geography, Louis Guglielmi, 40
Metropolitan Museum of Art, 115, 119
Midtown Galleries, 95, 125, 129
Morning, Zoltan Sepeshy, 129
Motif photographs, 9, 14, 70, 71, 145
Movement, pictorial, 19, 69, 123
 picture plane and, 23
Moya del Pino, Jose, 117
Murdock Collection, 50
Music, time in, 19

Namuth, Hans, photograph, 68
Nature, Andrews on, 55
 Arnautoff on, 57
 art and, 13
 artist and, 17
 Arthur on, 59
 Blackburn on, 61
 Bohrod on, 63
 Botton on, 65
 Bouché on, 67
 Brook on, 69
 Cikovsky on, 70
 copy of, 18
 Cowles on, 75
 defined, 17
 Delacroix on, 65
 Dodd on, 77
 Etnier on, 79
 Fausett on, 81
 Karfiol on, 91
 Klitgaard on, 97
 Knaths on, 99
 Loran on, 109
 Lucioni on, 111
 Lurie on, 113
 Osver on, 121

painter's attitude toward, 9, 14
Peirce on, 125
Philipp on, 123
Sepeshy on, 129
Spruance on, 131
Tam on, 133
three dimensions, 18
Wengenroth on, 38
Wessels on, 137
Neumann, J. B., Collection, 33
Newark Museum, 41
NEW YORK, Joseph Stella, 41
Nocturne, Arthur Osver, 121
Non-objective painting, 17, 142, 143
Northern Terrain, Reuben Tam, 133

Observer, picture and, 14
Obsolete Structure, Louis Guglielmi, 85
O'Keeffe, Georgia, 119
Opposed diagonals, 21
   in pattern and space, 26
Order, in art, 14
Oregon Coast, Glenn Wessels, 137
Organization, in art forms, 18
Osver, Arthur, 121
Overlapping, space and, 18, 23

Painting, imagination in, 15
   limitations, 13
   two dimensions, 18
   words and, 13
Pattern, 69
   flatness, 24
   illustrated, 24, 25
   line directions in, 26
   space and, 25, 59
Patrick, photograph, 98
Peirce, Waldo, 124, 125
Penitente Country, John Haley, 87
Perspective, atmospheric, 57
   mechanical, 23
   pictorial space vs., 23
Philipp, Robert, 122, 123
Photographs, communicative, 15
   motif, 9, 14, 70, 71, 145
Pictorial space, 55, 69
   color and, 28
   copy of nature vs., 18
   horizons and, 79, 91
   illustrated, 18, 23, 25
   line directions in, 26
   pattern and, 25, 59
   perspective vs., 23
   vertical, 67
Picture plane, illustrated, 22
   movement and, 23

spatial effect of, 22
Pictures, observer and, 14
   story-telling, 19
   time in, 19
PICTURES, PAINTERS, AND YOU, Bethers, 9, 63, 95
Pino, Jose Moya del, 117
Pony Ride, Louis Bouché, 67
Primitive painters, 33
Protrusion, illustrated, 22

Raffo, Steve, 127
Ranchos Church, Georgia O'Keeffe, 119
Reality, Kuniyoshi on, 101
Red Summer Sun, Morris Blackburn, 61
Rehn Galleries, 97, 127
Rio Grande, Howard Cook, 73
Rock Equilibrium, Erle Loran, 109
Roman Walls, Eric Isenburger, 89
Rooftops No. 1, David Fredenthal, 49
Rosenberg, Paul, Gallery, 99
Rules in art, 14

Sadness, curving directions and, 21
Salpeter, Harry, Gallery, 103
Salt Walter Farm, Hazard Durfee, 42, 43
Schuman, Mr. and Mrs. Seymour, Collection, 121
Seeing, Matisse on, 15
Sepeshy, Zoltan, 128, 129
Shape, effect of on pictures, 20
Shinnecock Hills, Nicolai Cikovsky, 71
Space, actual, 18
   Guglielmi on, 40
   pictorial (*see* Pictorial space)
Speed, horizontals and, 21
Spruance, Benton, 130, 131
Stability, 21
Stella, Joseph, 41
Stieglitz Collection, Metropolitan Museum of Art, 115, 119
Stieglitz, Marcel, Collection, 123
Still Life with the Spinet, Jean de Botton, 64
Story-telling pictures, 19
Subjective line, 67, 69
Subject matter, 15, 142, 143
   Botton on, 64
   Franck on, 37
Summer Rain, David Fredenthal, 51
Symbols, emotion and, 20

Tam, Reuben, 132, 133
Taylor, John, 134, 135
Textures, effect of, 28
Thought, 28

Three Graces, Luigi Lucioni, 111
Tide Wash, Karl Knaths, 99
Times Square, Frederick Franck, 35
Times Square, Israel Litwak, 33
Tolbert, Mildred, photograph, 106
Tower, The, John Taylor, 135
Trees, Sea and Rocks, Jose Moya del Pino, 117
Triangles, in pattern and space, 26-27
  strength, 21
  unstable, 21

Unification, 24

Valley Below, The, Ward Lockwood, 107
Values, color and, 61
  defined, 28
  textures and, 28
Van Diemen–Lilienfeld Galleries, 35, 37
Variety, in art, 14
  in nature, 17

Verticals, dignity, 21
  in pattern and space, 26

Wengenroth, Stow, 39
Wessels, Glenn, 136, 137
Wichita Art Museum, 50
Wilson, Sol, 138, 139
Wind and Sun, David Fredenthal, 52
Winter Moonlight, Benton Spruance, 131
Woolworth Building, New York, No. 3, John Marin, 115
Words, painting and, 13

Xceron, Jean, 143

Yale University, Collection of American Literature, 9, 115

Zerbe, Karl, 141

Books that Live

The Norton imprint on a book means that in the publisher's estimation it is a book not for a single season but for the years.

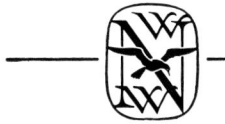

W · W · NORTON & CO · INC ·